Mysterious Mexico: A History of Ghosts, Legends, and Perplexing Places across the Mexican States

By Gustavo Vazquez-Lozano & Charles River Editors

Depiction of the founding myth of Mexico-Tenochtitlan from the Codex Mendoza

About Charles River Editors

Charles River Editors is a boutique digital publishing company, specializing in bringing history back to life with educational and engaging books on a wide range of topics. Keep up to date with our new and free offerings with this 5 second sign up on our weekly mailing list, and visit Our Kindle Author Page to see other recently published Kindle titles.

We make these books for you and always want to know our readers' opinions, so we encourage you to leave reviews and look forward to publishing new and exciting titles each week.

Introduction

Mural by Diego Rivera depicting the view from the Tlatelolco markets into Mexico-Tenochtitlan, one of the largest cities in the world at the time

Mysterious Mexico

At a time in antiquity when most of Europe was covered with forests and wandering tribes, Mexico had already developed complex civilizations, beginning with the Olmecs and followed by the Maya, a civilization with advanced knowledge of medicine, engineering and astronomy. The Maya calculated the precession of the equinoxes and cycles of the Pleiades, on which they based their year, since they believed they had come from that constellation. The last, and perhaps most famous, great civilization before the arrival of the Europeans was the Aztecs.

With so many ancient peoples whose influence, beliefs, and modifications to the landscape extend to the present day, Mexico is fertile land for legends, ghosts, surprising places, and mysteries. A belief in communing with things that lie beyond (stars, constellations, and life after death), mysticism, and apparitions are intimately woven into the colorful fabric of the Mexican nation, to the point that a metaphysical event (the apparition of the Virgin of Guadalupe) is considered by many as one of the founding elements of the nation. Our Lady of Guadalupe has an eerie counterpart, another woman who appeared around the same time: La Llorona, the weeping woman. If the content of the former vision is loving and conciliatory, the latter is full of regret and agony.

La Llorona is just the first of a long procession of even less benign ghosts. For many years, human sacrifices and endless cruelties were committed in present-day Mexico City. People across the country believe that a legion of ghostly voices—if one believes in ghosts as a byproduct of repetition, remembrance and re-experience of tragic memories—can still heard in the cities and valleys of Mexico. After all, archaeologists have found evidence of chilling human sacrifices in the Mexican capital, proof that the ancient inhabitants honored their gods by decapitating the bodies of their prisoners and putting their bleeding heads on a stick. Several sites have been found, and the largest one was unearthed in ancient Tenochtitlan (now Mexico City), which may contain up to 60,000 human skulls.

Mexico´s territory was relatively unknown until the beginning of the 20th century, even for its own people, as many of its ruins and natural wonders were out of reach or buried under thick jungles. It wasn´t until the development of the railroad at the turn of the 20th century that this vast country (the world's 14th largest) began to reveal its secrets. Once Mexico was pacified, the interest in Mayan and Aztec ruins and the strange stories that circulated in the villages brought dozens of archaeologists, anthropologists, photographers and historians from all over the world.

From that point, the nation was able to show its charms and mysteries to its own people and to strangers. The south kept memories of a race that talked to the stars, the center possessed ghosts filled with regret and resentment, and the north teemed with places that only a science fiction writer could imagine. The result is a collection of the most surprising, mysterious, and terrifying aspects of Mexico, including magical places, puzzles of history, and strange beings and apparitions. Mexico is a mystical country where everyday people have learned to live with their ghosts, old and new. As Octavio Paz, the Literature Nobel Prize winner, once said, "One of the most remarkable traits of the Mexican character is its willingness to contemplate horror—the Mexican is even familiar and complacent in his dealings with it."

Mysterious Mexico: A History of Ghosts, Legends, and Perplexing Places across the Mexican States covers the mysteries and oddities of the region, with a sampling of strange, unexplained, and just plain odd stories from Mexico that have fascinated people in and around the area for centuries. Along with pictures of important people, places, and events, you will learn about Mysterious Mexico like never before.

The Mayan Traveler from Space

Many ancient civilizations have influenced and inspired people in the 21st century. The Greeks and Romans continue to fascinate the West today. But of all the world's civilizations, few have intrigued people more than the Mayans, whose culture, astronomy, language, and mysterious disappearance all continue to captivate people. In 2012 especially, there was a renewed focus on the Mayans, whose advanced calendar led many to speculate the world would end on the same date the Mayan calendar ends. The focus on the "doomsday" scenario, however, has overshadowed the Mayans' true contribution to astronomy, language, sports, and art.

Ubiquitous in popular and scholarly descriptions of Maya civilization is the word enigma. In spite of tremendous advances in archaeology that continue to reveal more and more information on the highly developed Maya civilization of Mesoamerica, there remain many unanswered questions. Two examples of significant unresolved questions concerning the Maya illustrate the serious holes in scholars' knowledge. Despite the existence of their civilization in South America for thousands of years, historians and archaeologists still cannot explain where the Maya came from or exactly why their civilization collapsed.

Why have these questions continued to go unanswered? These unsolved mysteries surrounding the Maya civilization persist in large measure due to the efficiency of the Spanish in eradicating the remnants of Maya culture. And unlike the Aztecs, the disappearance of the Mayans cannot be clearly traced to a series of battles. By the early 16th century the Spanish conquistadors, along with the colonists and zealous propagators of the faith who followed the likes of Cortés and Pizarro, set out to systematically destroy the indigenous Maya civilization of the Yucatan that was already in decline even before their arrival. The land-grabbing colonists used the natives as virtual slave labor and pillaged their cities, while enthusiastic Catholic baptizers did their best to erase their heathen beliefs.

While the blame for the loss of much of the Mayan culture can be heaped upon the Spanish, much of what is known about life in a Maya community comes from the writings of the Provincial of the Franciscans in the Yucatan, Bishop Diego de Landa. His 1566 book, Relación de las cosas de Yucatán (An Account of the Affairs in the Yucatan), contains detailed observations on the culture of the Maya, including a record of their hieroglyphics and writing system. These have proved to be invaluable sources for those piecing together a picture of Mayan life. But Bishop Landa was also responsible for what in retrospect was an incalculable loss for the world. The Mayans' developed the only full language during the Mesoamerican period, but Landa and his Franciscan cohorts confiscated a great number of books written in the Mayan language which they believed were full of heretical ideas and burned them all. Bishop Landa's well-intentioned bonfire of books left the world with only four extant Maya manuscripts and a 1558 record written in Latin characters of Maya cosmology called the Popol Vuh, or book of the people preserving oral tradition of the K'iche Maya of Guatemala.

The Maya's writings obviously weren't the only things lost to history. In the years after the conquest of the Maya some of their cities were mined by the colonists for building materials. A spectacular example of this is took place at Izamal, where Bishop Landa's Monastery of San Antonio de Padua was constructed with stones reused from a Maya building. The Monastery itself, rising above the colonial town, sits on a plinth that is, in fact, a truncated Maya pyramid. Other Maya cities still inhabited in the period of conquest were abandoned and eventually obscured by jungle vegetation. Explorers in the jungle still find lost ruins of the Maya in Central America, and one incorrect story that made the rounds in 2011 speculated that Mayan ruins were found in North Georgia, a reflection of the interest and uncertainty still surrounding the Maya.

When the Europeans arrived in America, the jungle had all but devoured the Mayan ruins. To date, scholars have identified several magnificent buildings still covered by the thick jungle that sheltered them for more than a thousand years, but they are still not sure what exactly made the Mayans leave their cities so suddenly. The last Mayan inscription in the city of Palenque (in the state of Chiapas, southern Mexico) dates back to 799 and was found in a ceramic vessel. After that, there's nothing.

In the early 19th century, explorers and adventurers began to rediscover several Maya sites. Following the opinions of the colonists. who at the time perceived the contemporary Maya as unsophisticated and culturally impoverished, the explorers were initially convinced that these people could not have been responsible for such elaborate building projects. Given some of their similarities to the ancient civilizations in Europe and Egypt, they concluded that the Maya pyramids and other structures they discovered must have somehow been the work of Greeks, Romans, Egyptians or Indians from India. How exactly these Mayan city builders got to the region was explained by fanciful conjecture on cultural migration.

The many (and ongoing) accounts of discoveries of Mayan cities by archaeologists and explorers have only added to the mysteries of the Maya civilization, which in turn continue to fuel interest and speculation. Early archaeologists attributed names to the buildings in many sites based on assumptions as to their use, which has led to misleading descriptions that should be paid little attention. At Uxmal, today a very popular Yucatan tourist destination, there are buildings called the Nunnery and the Governor's Palace, both of which are based on quite fanciful ideas of the original purpose of the structures. At Chichén Itzá, the greatest Maya city in the Yucatan, one is taken by guides to a building called the Nunnery for no good reason other than the small rooms reminded the Spaniards of a nunnery back home. Similarly the great pyramid at Chichén Itzá is designated the El Castillo, the Castle, which it certainly is not, and the Observatory is called El Caracol, the Snail, for its spiral staircase. This kind of confusing naming of Maya structures had been abandoned at recently discovered sites and replaced with less colorful terms such as, for example, Temple 1, Temple II and so on at Tikal in Guatemala.

The Pyramid of the Magician at Uxmal and Building of the Iguana at Uxmal are perfect examples of fanciful but nonsensical names.

The Castle at Chichén Itzá

One spectacular discovery made by archeologists in the mid-20th century adds to the mystery of the Maya's abrupt disappearance. In 1952, Alberto Ruz Lhuillier discovered a secret passage in the Temple of the Inscriptions at Palenque that led to the tomb of Pakal, a ruler who had reigned for 67 years. That was an incredibly long time, which may explain why his people took special care with his burial. Pakal was buried with about a thousand pieces of jade. His skull was covered with a mask of the same material–the most precious for the Maya–along with shells and other precious stones. Currently, the pieces are in the National Museum of Anthropology in Mexico City, with the exception of the sarcophagus cover, which remains inside the pyramid´s secret chamber.

Jan Harenburg's picture of the Temple of the Inscriptions

The art covering the sarcophagus is, to say the least, astonishing: it´s a five-ton stone decorated with an enigmatic illustration. According to historians, the image shows Pakal about to embark on a long journey from the valley of the living to the land of the dead, represented by a monster´s jaws. Above the king is the Tree of Life and the center of the universe, plus a heavenly bird that represents paradise.

An illustration of the art on the sarcophagus

On the other hand, by using modern visual references, a completely different interpretation can emerge, because the image in Pakal's tomb has all of the traits of a man riding a module or a capsule with what appears to be flames being expelled from the bottom of the module, like the engines of a rocket. Moreover, his hands seem to be on the controls, buttons, and levers, and in lieu of a mask, a respirator covers Pakal's nose. In the UFO craze of the 1970s and 1980s, the image rose to fame as the so-called "Astronaut of Palenque." According to Erich von Däniken, the sarcophagus "depicts the whole arsenal of space-flight paraphernalia: supply systems, helmets, transmitters, an observer in satellite, and oxygen apparatus." Von Däniken is not exactly a respected member of the academic community, but it's unquestionably tantalizing to look at the image of Palenque, play with the possibility, and at least wonder about it.

Another mystery that augments Pakal´s story is that, according to the inscriptions, the ruler was 80 at the time of his death, but the skeleton had the teeth and bones of a person 40 years younger. This led some to speculate that there was someone else buried in the pyramid.

Either way, anyone interested in the Maya and the story would be best served to go to Mexico and see the image with their own eyes, even though it will have to be a reproduction since the original sarcophagus in the pyramid, which was visited every year by more than half a million people, was forever closed to the public in 2007.

Montezuma´s Treasure

"Among these temples there is one which far surpasses all the rest, whose grandeur of architectural details no human tongue is able to describe; for within its precincts, surrounded by a lofty wall, there is room enough for a town of five hundred families." – Hernán Cortés

Regardless of the precise population count, when the Spanish conquistador Hernán Cortés and his men arrived in the Aztec capital of Tenochtitlán, it was probably larger than any European city of the era. Bernal Díaz, who accompanied Cortés, described the reaction of the Spanish soldiers as they first approached the great city: "We saw so many cities and villages built both on the water and on dry land, and a straight, level causeway (to Tenochtitlan), we couldn't resist our admiration. It was like the enchantments in the book of Amadis (de Gaula, a popular Spanish chivalric romance of the late middle ages), because of the high towers, pyramids and other buildings, all of masonry, which rose from the water. Some of our soldiers asked if what we saw was not a dream." This was the first great urban civilization that the Spaniards, who had initially come to the Americas seeking the rich and sophisticated kingdoms of Asia, encountered in the New World. It is a remarkable fact that within less than two years of their first arrival there, Tenochtitlán as they had found it would be in ruins.

When Hernan Cortés and Emperor Montezuma II greeted each other in Tenochtitlan in 1519, one of the most important moments in the history of mankind took place. According to Yuval Noah Harari in his book, *Sapiens*, it was the moment when the planet ceased to be a group of isolated civilizations and became a global village. At the time, however, Cortés was not interested in inaugurating globalization or diplomacy, much less commerce. "We Spaniards have a disease of the heart," he explained to the ancient Mexicans, "that only gold can cure." And Montezuma, the emperor of vast dominions in what is now Mexico and part of Central America, had the metal in abundance. To flatter his visitor, he presented him with exquisite pieces of gold, among them a colossal disk made of pure gold representing the sun. Little did he suspect that instead of pleasing him, he was only stirring up the conqueror´s ambition. Bernal Díaz del Castillo, an eyewitness of that meeting, offered a description of Montezuma: "He was about 40 years old, of good height and well-proportioned, slender and spare of flesh, not very swarthy, but of the natural color and shade of an Indian. He did not wear his hair long, but so as just to cover his ears, his scanty black beard was well-shaped and thin. His face was somewhat long, but cheerful, and he had good eyes and showed in his appearance and manner both tenderness and, when necessary, gravity."

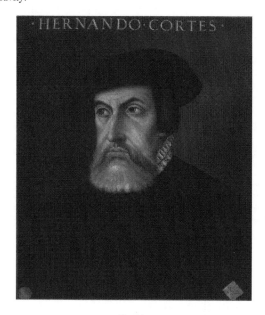

Cortés

A contemporary depiction of the meeting

Many have wondered why an apparently hostile army was treated with such hospitality, especially after a previous massacre at Cholula. One theory is that Moctezuma simply did not imagine that such a small force could be a threat to his enormous city, and once the strangers were ensconced in the city, he may have reasoned, they were trapped and would have great difficulty escaping.

If this was his intention, the Aztec ruler severely underestimated his opponent. Not long after arriving in Tenochtitlán, apparently prompted by a report that his men back in Veracuz had been attacked by the Aztecs, Cortés took Moctezuma hostage in his own palace. The ruler showed little resistance, allowing the Spaniards to plunder the royal storehouses of gold. For several months, Cortés essentially ruled Tenochtitlán through the authority of his captive, not establishing decisive control there but biding his time until a more forceful move could be taken.

However, Cortés still had the authorities of his own government to deal with as well. In April 1520, a Spanish expedition of around 1,000 men under the command of Pánfilo de Narváez was sent out by Governor Velázquez from Cuba with orders to subdue Cortés. Here again Cortés was severely outnumbered, but his ruthlessness won out. Leaving Tenochtitlán and heading for the coast, Cortés feigned a desire to enter into peace talks, holding out a promise of consensual submission to the governor's authority. All the while, he was planning to attack and sending messengers to Narváez's camp with bribes and promises of rewards if they mutinied against their appointed leader. Narváez was unprepared when Cortés and his men descended on the encampment fully armed and ready to fight. He was forced to surrender and fell captive to his enemy, who left him imprisoned in Veracruz while leading off a large contingent of his soldiers back toward Tenochtitlán. It is an interesting fact that Cortés did not reserve his treacherous disregard for basic honesty for his interactions with the natives. He behaved with similar callousness toward his own people, albeit with much less brutality, but even that might have been only because he did not have to resort to brute force.

While Cortés was dealing with fellow Spaniards, the group of Spaniards in Tenochtitlán had meanwhile carried out a massacre as shocking and probably with more even bloodshed than the one in Cholula. Cortés's lieutenant Pedro de Alvarado was immediately responsible for planning and ordering the attack, but it is not clear whether he was acting under orders from his superior or on his own initiative. Some speculate that Cortés deliberately planned for it to occur during his absence so that he could claim to have been uninvolved. The occasion of the massacre was the festival of Toxatl, which celebrated the god Tezcatlipoca and was probably the largest and most important of all Aztec feast days. The nobles and priests of the city were gathered in the courtyard of the great Templo Mayor, which could only be accessed through four narrow entrances. With his small group of Spaniards, Alvarado sealed off the exits and in the midst of the celebration, entered into the courtyard and began slaughtering the gathered Aztecs, all of them unarmed. They are thought to have killed thousands, possibly as many as eight thousand, that day, primarily using swords, spears, and knives. As in Cholula, the perpetrators later claimed that they had gotten wind of a plot against them by the Aztecs; they also claimed that they were acting to prevent the participants in the festival from carrying out rituals involving human sacrifice and cannibalism.

Pedro de Alvarado

It's no surprise that the Spaniards would use the Aztec human sacrifice rituals as a pretext to justify their aggression. More is known about Aztec religious practices than any other aspect of their culture, mostly because the major element in the public ceremonies was focused on human sacrifice. The rituals were apparently so gruesome that they horrified even the Spanish, who were not exactly known for being gentle when it came to war and religious fervor.

When Cortés and his forces got back to Tenochtitlan, they found the city's streets deserted and the population openly hostile. What ensued was a kind of prototype of urban guerrilla warfare. In the tight, enclosed spaces of the city, the Spaniards' horses were of little advantage, and their weapons could not be fired effectively. Within a short period, it became clear that they had lost their advantage, and they were running low on food and artillery. Cortés's gambit was to have Montezuma, still his captive, speak to his people, ostensibly in the hope of a further reconciliation. Having ascended to the roof of his palace to speak to the assembled Aztecs, Montezuma was killed under circumstances that still remain uncertain. The Spaniards subsequently claimed that he was stoned to death by his own people, while the native accounts mainly assert that the Spaniards themselves killed the emperor by literally stabbing him in the back while he tried to speak. Both scenarios are relatively plausible, but the latter explanation certainly fits with Cortés' style.

The retreat that followed after Montezuma's death has become known as the *Noche triste* ("sad night," "night of sorrow"), although the Aztecs were presumably not sorry to see the Spaniards go or even terribly sorry for the loss of their ineffectual ruler. Cortés and his men, knowing they were badly outnumbered and had little chance of surviving open combat in the city, chose to flee after sending a false message of truce to their enemies. They fled in the middle of the night, aiming for the most deserted causeway leading out of the city and across the lake, but the retreat still went disastrously. It began to rain heavily, thunderstorms added to their consternation, and all out chaos ensued when they were attacked by large numbers of their opponents, who had been alerted to their movements. Many of the Spaniards were weighted down with gold and other loot from the city and drowned when they tried to swim away from the causeway, while others were simply killed by the attackers. All in all, hundreds of them did not escape the city alive, leaving the force greatly diminished.

By the time Cortés reached the shores of the lake, he had lost most of his army and much of the treasure he and his men had taken from Montezuma's palace. His initial plan to take control of the Aztec empire by stealth, keeping Montezuma on the throne as a nominal leader while ruling from behind the scenes, had failed disastrously. Now he would need to try a different and far more dramatic strategy.

By the time the Aztecs sent out expeditionary forces to attack the Spaniards in the Fall of 1520, the Spaniards had gathered an impressive array of support from native allied forces, and their own resources had augmented thanks to a growing trickle of soldiers, horses, and artillery arriving from the Gulf of Mexico. Still, the army that finally gathered to re-enter the Valley of Mexico toward the end of that same year was less than 5% Spanish, and it is unlikely that most of the native soldiers who participated regarded themselves as under Cortés's command. The traditional view of the "Spanish Conquest" thus needs to be revised. Although the Spaniards ultimately derived the most benefit from the war against the Aztecs, most of the participants in the successful campaign were neither Spanish nor conquerors: they were pursuing an agenda that would ostensibly increase their city's share of regional power. A further and equally crucial actor in the ultimate triumph of the Spaniards was one of the diseases they had brought with them from Europe: smallpox. By late 1520, a devastating outbreak of the illness had ravaged Tenochtitlán, killing perhaps 40% of its population.

Finally, in July 1521, the Spaniards and their allies managed to gain a foothold on the island, and proceeded to make their way through the city, razing structures to the ground to prevent ambushes. Worn down by illness, starvation, thirst, and relentless arquebus and cannon attacks, the Aztecs held out until August 13, 1521, the day Emperor Cuahtemoc was captured. He reportedly surrendered directly to Cortés, but his surrender was not recognized and he was taken prisoner and ultimately executed. The total numbers are uncertain, but Aztec casualties from the siege, including the deaths of warriors in battle and deaths from illness, starvation, and massacres of civilians, reached the hundreds of thousands. In the latest stage of their campaign, the

Spaniards had lost perhaps 500 and native allies had perished in the tens of thousands. Within less than two years, the Aztec empire had been destroyed, the population decimated, and the great capital left in ruins. Cortés proceeded to take credit for the entire enterprise, but in reality his success was highly dependent on the enormous assistance he received from his local allies. Perhaps more than a great military strategist, he had again shown himself to be a consummate politician.

One of the most fascinating aspects of Montezuma's legend is the large treasure he supposedly collected during his 18 years as emperor. This should not be surprising, considering that during his reign, the Aztec Empire reached its apex, and Montezuma demanded from conquered nations a large tribute to be paid in gold, jade, exotic feathers, other jewels, and animals, such as jaguars and eagles. From the beginning, Cortés and his people were desperate to gather all the gold they could, and while they held the emperor captive, they demanded it every day. When Cortés returned to the coast to combat an insurrection, Montezuma "ordered his buildings stripped of their gold, silver, and jewels. Gold ingots were taken from the treasury and seven caravans of one hundred porters, each carrying approximately 60 pounds of gold, was sent to the north." (Childress, 1992).

While there is still uncertainty surrounding Montezuma's death, it's even less clear where the fabulous treasure he ordered taken out of Tenochititlan was hidden, and the mystery has never been solved. Some believe the gold was buried in the Sierra Madre in northwestern Mexico, and even as far away as Utah and Arizona, one of the favorite sites of treasure hunters (nowhere else in the United States has as many references to Montezuma as Arizona). In the American Southwest, geographical landmarks abound with names like Montezuma's Castle, Montezuma's Well, Montezuma's Head, and two different sites in the mountains called Montezuma's Peak. Others speculate that the caravans were divided into several parties and that the treasure was placed in two different spots.

It's also possible that a large part of the treasure remained in Mexico City, since there were not enough means to extract such an amount of gold. If so, at least a part of it may have been found in 1981, when a group of archaeologists announced to the president of Mexico that they had discovered a considerable amount of gold under the building of the Bank of Mexico. "This is the first (part of the) discovery of Montezuma's treasure," the proud Jose Lopez Portillo (a president remembered as someone given to hyperbole) told the press. The team of archaeologists made an itemization: "The pieces recovered...were initially two gold bars, fifteen pieces of gold work, two clay beads and twenty-three gold bars of recent casting, with different weights and measures. However, after repeated confrontations between the accused, who had declared that they had delivered all the pieces, they confessed to having still in their possession twenty-three more pieces of goldwork." Ironically, this treasure – or at least that part of it – vanished, and no one knows who took it home. If those archaeologists found more gold in 1981, only President Lopez Portillo knew it, and unfortunately, he took the secret to his grave.

Portillo

The Virgin of Guadalupe

"In the beginning when the Christian faith had just arrived here in the land that today is called New Spain, in many ways the heavenly lady, the consummate Virgin Saint Mary, cherished, aided and defended the local people so that they might entirely give themselves and adhere to the faith . . in order that they might invoke her fervently and trust in her fully, she saw fit to reveal herself for the first time to two [Indian] people here."

No other artwork in the world is comparable to the Virgin of Guadalupe. What makes this painting unique —located in the Basilica of Guadalupe, north of Mexico City— is not precisely its artistic quality, as is the case with the *Mona Lisa* by Leonardo or *The Kiss* by Gustav Klimt, nor its place in the evolution of painting. It clearly does not constitute a landmark in art history, and the most visited painting in the world is certainly not the summit or the harbinger of a new aesthetic movement, like Dali´s melting watches or Van Gogh´s *Starry Night*. In fact, for some, the execution of the image is coarse and all its elements fit well known techniques. For others, it´s merely a copy of a sculpture of the Virgin found in Spain.

What distinguishes the Virgin of Guadalupe of Mexico is her universality: unlike any work of art in the world, it can be recognized by any local; it´s certainly the most ubiquitous symbol in her country. It would be difficult to find a Mexican who cannot name her. Likewise, it would be complicated to find one who hasn´t been at least once in his or her life before the image at the Basilica, either reluctantly or filled with devotion. The other thing that makes the Virgin of Guadalupe incomparable is her power to unite her nation, something that has been widely demonstrated throughout history. At different moments, and raised by different hands, the Virgin of Guadalupe (never the original painting) has led the troops that changed the history of the territory now known as Mexico. Not even a few hours had passed after the start of the War of Independence when the rebel army was already carrying the image of Guadalupe; in the twentieth century the image was present at the indigenous rebellion in Chiapas in 1994 and also materialized during the Mexican "perestroika" of 2000, which ended the single-party regime that had lasted for seven decades. Going further back, during Mexico´s Conquest, Hernán Cortés carried an image of the Virgin that, to the disinterested observer, is obviously the prototype of the Mexican Madonna.

For some, Guadalupe is the work of a talented Indian painter, and this work was retouched and embellished by others in later centuries. The majority of scholars note how the image "appeared" at a very convenient time in Mexico´s history, when evangelization functioned as the ideological arm of the material conquest of the Aztec empire. There are even reasons to wonder whether the image currently on display in Mexico City is the same as in the 17th century since it is known from testimonies of the time that Mary had a crown on her head. That means if it´s the same, at the very least it´s been retouched, doctored and tampered with again.

Conversely, for the believers, the image was miraculously stamped on the tilma or cloak of a man named Juan Diego. Among the latter are most of the 17 million persons who visit the original every year in Mexico City, which makes it the most visited painting in the country, and certainly the world. By comparison, the Mona Lisa at the Louvre in Paris receives six million visitors per year.

Historical fact or pious legend, Mexicans don´t take the story as a joke. Until recently a saying circulated in Mexico that only two things were untouchable in the country: the President and the Virgin of Guadalupe. That said, the Lady of Tepeyac[i] remains, for practical purposes, a symbol that has to be handled with care. On several occasions, art exhibitions that have reinterpreted or distorted her image have been suspended or boycotted. In 1987 an art exhibition of a Guatemalan artist in Mexico City was shut out because his paintings showed the Virgin with Marilyn Monroe´s face. In 2002, a film by Carlos Carrera, *The Crime of Father Amaro*, had a scene of a young couple making love over a carpet with the image of the Virgin of Guadalupe. The movie unleashed the fury of millions of Catholics across the country.[ii] However, it´s not uncommon for those in prison for violent crimes to have the image tattooed on their backs for protection, and nobody feels offended, nor by the fact that some drug traffickers carve her image on the gold handles of their revolvers.

What nobody questions —believers, skeptics or atheists— is that the Virgin of Guadalupe has been the most important symbol, religious or not, in Mexico's history, a kind of non-official flag. Her influence has spread even to the Mexican diaspora, where it has become a sign of identity, pride and resistance among undocumented immigrants in the United States. For Mexicans, it's not necessary to be religious to believe in the power of the Virgin of Guadalupe as a unifying symbol and embodiment of national identity. In only a few years, the image will reach the respectable age of half a millennium, if it was indeed painted in the traditionally assigned date. 500 years later, how much it is verifiable and how much of it is legend? What social role has the icon had, and how has it impacted Mexican politics? In the end, to tell the story of the brown-skinned Virgin, neither Indian nor Spaniard, is to observe the birth and development of a nation called Mexico, erected by the European sword and cross over the ruins of the Aztec empire.

Of course, few people agree on everything regarding the Virgin of Guadalupe. It seems beyond dispute that during Zumárraga's administration a small chapel (ermita) was built to the Virgin Mary, without any special name, on the Tepeyac hill.[iii] At least that's what missionary Juan de Torquemada wrote in his *Monarquía Indiana*, some 70 years later: "Our first clerics (...) decided to put a church and temple at the foot of these mountains of Tlaxcallan, in a town called Chiauhtempa (...) In Tianhuizmanalco they built the house for St. John the Baptist; and in Tonantzin, next to Mexico City, one to the most holy Virgin (...) and in these three places festivals are celebrated."

As is the case with other visions of Mary, the Guadalupe apparitions took place at a critical time in the nation, as the dust had barely settled and the blood had barely dried after the fall of Tenochtitlan. Although there is no official figure for the inhabitants of the Aztec Empire — estimates range from 6 million to 25 million — what is certain is that a few decades later, epidemics and forced labor eradicated almost all the population, leaving only approximately a million people. The epidemic "was so huge that it ruined and destroyed almost all the land," wrote Juan de Torquemada, "Mexico was left almost deserted."

It is in the midst of this confusion and disappointment that the cult of Guadalupe begins.[iv] Many historians and critical Catholics have pointed out that the apparition of a mixed-race Virgin was suspiciously timely and convenient, right at the moment when the evangelization began from Mexico to the whole continent. This process, called the Spiritual Conquest (because it occurred at the same time and sometimes in competition with the material conquest of America), with the Virgin of Guadalupe at the forefront, "seems to have aided considerably in the easing of tensions between Indians and Spaniards in the 1530s." (Leatham, 1989).

When the devotion was well established in the mid-16th century, some sectors of the church began to oppose it because, in their opinion, it was taking an improper turn. However, despite this opposition, its rapid expansion shows that the indigenous population had reasons to defend it, and moreover that the cult must have been supported by other quarters of the emerging Mexican church.

In the late 18th century, a couple of decades before the War of Independence, a glorification of Mexico's indigenous past began to emerge, fueled by the Jesuits against Spain. The Virgin of Guadalupe was paramount in the attempt to recover the golden past and "real Mexican spirit," and it spontaneously became a symbol of independence. Father Miguel Hidalgo, the initiator of the movement, took an image of the Virgin of Guadalupe as a flag, put it in front of his people's army, and had another sewn on his chest (to shoot him would be to shoot the Virgin). At his trial, he acknowledged that the image had attracted multitudes: "On September 16 (…) when we passed through Atotonilco I took an image of Guadalupe and put it in the hands of a man to carry it in front of the people who accompanied him, and the first and riotous regiments that formed later, as well as the crowds, took the same image of Guadalupe of Arms." Hidalgo also said he had done this because he had "knowledge of the devotion they (Indians) had to this holy image."

In some respects, the story of the Virgin of Guadalupe is not out of the ordinary, as reported apparitions of the Virgin, especially to humble people, shepherds, and children, have occurred in many places in the world, especially Mediterranean countries. However, while the image of the Virgin of Guadalupe and the canvas (actually made of maguey fibers) have some attributes that many believe are miraculous —the conservation of the maguey fibers for almost half a millennium is a miracle in and of itself—nothing has aroused the interest of believers more than the woman´s eyes, where several people and faces can supposedly be seen under a microscope, including full scenes.

It all began in 1929, when Alfonso Marcué, the official photographer of the Basilica, thought he saw a face in the Virgin´s right eye. When he commented on his discovery, the ecclesiastical authorities ordered him to stay silent about it. In 1951, a sketcher named Carlos Salinas had the same impression while examining a photograph of the Virgin´s face. Thereafter, several ophthalmologists examined the painting´s corneas, which measure approximately 8 mm across, amplifying them 12,000X. One of the most recent studies was made by Jose Aste Tönsmann, an expert with twenty years' experience at IBM in image digitalization. According to Tönsmann, he found up to 13 human figures, including a family, Mexico´s first bishop, his interpreter Zumárraga, Juan Diego, and a black woman.

Although the idea is not new, in the mid-20th century there arose the notion that the name Guadalupe and the image itself had to be decoded in indigenous terms, meaning the painting was not just a religious icon but part of an Indian codex.[v] As such, the image was supposedly full of symbols that formed a complete catechism, one that only an inhabitant of pre-Conquest Mexico could decipher without the help of an evangelizer. Scholar Patricia Harrington (1988) states, "For the Indians, it was natural to place a goddess above one of her primary symbols, the moon. If the Spaniards had destroyed the solar cult of Huitzilopochtli and human sacrifice, this new incarnation revealed that the lunar goddess had overshadowed the solar god for a time and ushered in a new age." Virgilio Elizondo proposed that the stars in the mantle announced to the Indians the end of a civilization and the beginning of a new one. Helen Behrens wrote in 1952 that "the stars meant that Mary commands the firmament," and another scholar linked the starry mantle with the "star-skirt" of the Aztec mother goddess, Tonantzin. They may have been looking too hard, and just like those who see a star map on the mantle, they found what they wanted to see. The studies of Callahan in 1979 showed that almost all those elements are later additions, although the discussion seems to have no end (one argued that "Callahan miscalculated the opening of the lens of his camera").

For skeptics, the explanation is simple: a phenomenon known as pareidolia. The same phenomenon that makes people "see" men in the moon or faces on the trunks of trees makes them find bishops and Indians in the enlargements of the painting´s eyes.

Whatever the case, the Virgin of Guadalupe is clearly an influence that far exceeds the religious sphere. The image has the ability to communicate effectively with no need of explicit messages, and the power to move consciences. These days, the Mexican Church does not insist too heavily on the supernatural quality of the image; in fact, it has repeatedly made clear that it´s not required of any Catholic to believe in the apparitions or the painting since they belong to the realm of private revelation. It´s not a dogma. This may be because the Church figures that one day — in the spirit of the first bishop of Mexico, Juan de Zumárraga — it may want to insist that faith should not be based on external ritualism. Perhaps the Church is anticipating that another definitive study will reveal purely human origins. But this doesn´t bother Mexicans, because the image's bonding power and identity is already beyond what any "scientific" analysis could prove.

The Death of Emperor Maximilian really die in Mexico?

Portrait of the emperor circa 1864

Once upon a time, when a Civil War threatened to fracture the U.S., there was a monarchy south of the Rio Grande. That kingdom was called Mexico. It had a magnificent castle, a beautiful princess and a tall, handsome prince; he was noble and idealistic, he had fire in his heart, but he was weak and gullible. A fool, some would say. One day, when he was still a teenager, he wrote, "Ambition is like the balloonist. To some extent, the rise is nice and he does enjoy a splendid view and a vast landscape. But when he rises more, vertigo occurs, the air becomes thin and the risk of a big fall increases." With this parable, the Austrian Archduke Maximilian of Hapsburg inadvertently predicted the destiny to which he would bravely ride, despite the warnings and the sweet talkers. In any case, he followed his heart´s mandate. And Charlotte, the princess, was "one of the most cultured and beautiful" in Europe. Since she was a girl she'd known that one day she would become a queen or an empress.

When it was first hinted that they would be offered the crown of Mexico, she was 22 and he was 28, and they were surrounded by the intrigue and ambition of their own brothers, who could not wait to have them removed from the picture. So when, three years later, the couple received the official diplomatic mission which affirmed Mexico required their presence, the proposition was like a fairy tale come true. In the imagination of the era, Mexico was the distant paradise described by the great geographer Alexander von Humboldt: thick jungles and forests, steaming volcanoes, copious gold and silver mines, infinite beaches and exotic birds. "The most dangerous worldview is the worldview of those who have not viewed the world," the Prussian explorer had written, and Max believed it in all sincerity and contemplated the adventure with the eyes of his soul.

In Mexico, the reality was different from the imagination. It was too late by the time they realized they had been seduced by sirens, specifically the siren sitting upon the throne of France, Napoleon III. The zealous emperor frowned at the expansion of the US and the Protestant, Anglo-Saxon race. But there were also the vast territories of northern Mexico to consider, the gold and silver mines, plus Napoleon's vague idea of rebuilding the Latin race and culture in the Americas. With that in mind, he brought two puppets to his global stage, Maximilian and Charlotte, and made sure they were told that the Mexican people would tender unto them a carpet of roses as soon as they saw their royal feet touch their land. In their dreams, Max of Austria and Charlotte of Belgium would become the saviors of the ancient empire of Montezuma, now unable to govern itself, and on the road to self-destruction. But Maximilian was not thinking of conquest and looting, as did his ancestor, Charles I of Spain, but in reconstruction and healing. It is not that he was guilty of arrogance, either. Sending a European monarch to the American continent sounds outrageous these days, but at the time, it was common for the kings of England, Belgium, Greece or Bulgaria to be of other nationalities. Still, Maximilian refused to accept the throne of Mexico until he was shown evidence that the Mexicans agreed. When he was shown a pretend plebiscite, he agreed on the dangerous adventure.

The tragedy of Maximilian and Charlotte was romantic and political. In Mexico's official history, the one recorded by the winners, they were an affront to independence and a symbol of European arrogance. For the monarchies of Europe, they are a sad and embarrassing memory, because of the abandonment, craftiness and treachery they lived through. Repentance came too late, as both were dead by then. One was buried in his grave, and the other had been driven insane. It's something that might have been penned by Shakespeare himself. Their story has been told many times, not only by historians, but also by filmmakers, novelists, and dramaturges. It all happened 150 years ago, but Mexicans—both inside and outside the country—still remember the lights and shadows of that time. Some look at the timeworn photographs with respect and sadness; others, with contempt. "The old nations have the disease of memories," Maximilian wrote, and Mexico, the country that he and his wife loved until their last breath, is already showing signs of aging.

Despite the official line, there is still mystery swirling over Maximilian's fate. In 1867, Mexico was engulfed in a civil war, and before the enemy's walls closed around Mexico City, Maximilian's advisers urged him to leave the capital and secure himself in Queretaro, a sheltered city thanks to the efforts of General Bazaine, who had fortified it a few years earlier. All the loyal troops gathered in that town, including Prince Felix Salm-Salm, a soldier of fortune who had participated in Prussia, the American Civil War, and now offered his sword in Maximilian's service.

At Queretaro, about 5,000 soldiers loyal to Maximilian faced off against Mariano Escobedo's 35,000, who overwhelmingly outnumbered their adversaries and mercilessly bombed the city. [vi] Escobedo was consumed by the hatred of everything foreign. After more than two months of hunger, siege and bombarding, the beleaguered were fed with only horsemeat and mules. They melted the church bells, pipes, and every piece of metal they found with which they made ammunition. Ultimately, it was not Escobedo's cannons that toppled the empire but betrayal, specifically from one of Maximilian's closest men, Miguel Lopez, who had frequently changed loyalties during his military career. Lopez allegedly negotiated with Escobedo to let him take the city in exchange for three thousand pesos of gold.

Escobedo

Lopez

The historical reconstruction of what happened next and the order of the events have been debated for years. After two months of siege, Maximilian's exhausted, hungry, and thirsty troops planned a desperate attempt to break the siege on May 16. Lopez, who was a man that held a position of trust with Maximilian, would lead the column. However, a few days before, he had a secret meeting with Mariano Escobedo in his camp to offer the surrender of the city without bloodshed. Lopez would deceive his troops, and clear the way for the republican army, which would pass through a loophole on the condition that Maximilian would not be immediately captured. [vii] On the 15th, Escobedo's army entered Querétaro through an arrowslit, with a column led by Lopez sent to take the imperialist headquarters.

Upon learning of the betrayal, Maximilian became furious, took his weapons, and said, "To get out of here or die is the only way." With a handful of men, he headed to a hill known as Cerro de las Campanas (The Hill of the Bells), where he was arrested by Escobedo himself, who triumphantly reported to Juárez that the city had fallen "by force," That wasn't technically true, but Escobedo wasn´t going to let a minor detail like that diminish his prestige.

Back in the capital, the Juárez government decreed that Maximilian was to suffer the death penalty by firing squad, despite the fact that the death penalty for political reasons was prohibited in Mexico. Many around the world begged for his life, including ambassadors, heads of state, members of European monarchies, and several prominent Mexicans, and also some who had opposed the Emperor. Even the famous writer Victor Hugo, who had admired Juárez, sent him a letter pleading, "Juárez, make civilization take this huge step. Juárez, abolish the death penalty in all the earth. Let the world see this wondrous thing: the Republic is holding his murderer, an emperor; when that is done, it discovers that he is a man, it lets him go and says: 'You are one of the people, like the others. Go!' This, Juárez, will be your second victory."

Princess Salm-Salm, the wife of the soldier of fortune who had planned Maximilian's escape from prison, traveled to San Luis Potosi where Juárez had been following the whole process. Upon her arrival, she threw herself at his feet and asked for clemency for the prisoner. "It causes me great pain, Madame, to see you like that on your knees," he replied, "but even if every king and queen were in your place, I couldn't spare his life. It isn't me who takes it from him, it is the people and the law who claim his life." Clearly, Juárez understood clemency as a sign of weakness.

As a result, on June 19, 1867, Maximilian and his two highest-ranking generals, Miguel Miramón and Tomas Mejía, were taken to Cerro de las Campanas, the same place where he had been arrested. A few days earlier, they'd informed him, perhaps to increase his pain, that Carlota had died in Europe, which wasn't true. The soldiers improvised an adobe wall on the hill. In the distance, 4,000 Republican soldiers stood and watched in silence as the carriage that brought Maximilian approached. When the emperor saw the hill, he exclaimed: "That's where I thought I would raise the flag of victory, and that is where I am going to die. Life is a comedy!"

Miramón

Mejia

As he climbed, he watched the crowd. A military command had just announced that if someone among the people said anything in the emperor's defense or begged for clemency for the prisoners, he or she would be shot there, too. If anyone uttered a prayer for the prisoners, they certainly did so in silence. Always the poet, Maximilian, watching the clear sky, broke the silence. "What a beautiful view. What a beautiful day to die," he said.

Good-natured until the end, he shook the hands of the firing squad and handed a gold coin to each soldier as a token of forgiveness. His last words were, "I will die for a just cause. I forgive everyone and ask all to forgive me too. My blood will seal the misfortunes of this country. Viva Mexico!" He was shot six times by incompetent soldiers and was thus still alive when he fell to the ground, next to a wooden cross someone had put on his left side. Blood gushed from his mouth as he babbled, possibly asking for a merciful stroke, and a soldier from the platoon approached him and shot him in the heart.

Now the absolute master of the city, Escobedo, still thirsting for revenge, wrote to Juárez: "I have, by the execution of these master traitors, made terror the order of the day everywhere. I have imposed large contributions on the rich, and confiscated their property and their all. I hope to see the blood of every foreigner split."

The Juárez government seized Maximilian's corpse and refused to deliver it to his family with due respect. The body lay naked and clumsily embalmed in the hospital church of San Andrés, Mexico City, where the president and his foreign minister went, incognito, to see him. It was the only time Juárez saw him in person. He examined the corpse for a moment. The only thing that came out of the mouth of the heroic defender of the law, the representative of dignity, the author of great maxims that have been carved in gold, was an unnecessarily insulting remark: "He was a tall man, but he didn't have a good body. His legs were too long and disproportionate. He had no talent, because although he had a long forehead, it was due to receding hair." The naked body was left hanging upside down from a hook for several days, until finally it was handed over to an Austrian delegation. When the temple became a place of pilgrimage for sentimental masses in honor of Maximilian, Juárez, in a fit of jealousy, ordered it to be demolished. Today there is a statue of Lerdo de Tejada in that place, the man who told the world the details of the unique encounter between Juárez, the living, and Maximilian, the dead.

In the wake of those chaotic events, a European merchant called Justo Armas arrived in El Salvador. The first certain proof of his presence in that country comes from 1871, when he donated some money for a religious celebration four years after Maximilian's death. This is where the mystery begins, because according to legend, Mr. Armas, a man of refined manners, eccentric and handsome, entered the country barefoot, in gratitude for the Virgin having saved him from a deadly danger. He promised never to reveal his true name. Justo Armas spoke several languages, including German, showed aristocratic manners, and taught classes on etiquette and protocol. Thanks to his good political education and knowledge of languages, he became an assistant to the Minister of Foreign Affairs of El Salvador. Found among his belongings were several objects from the court of Maximilian, such as tableware and spoons.

Armas

Salvadoran architect Rolando Dénike has hypothesized that Maximilian didn´t die in Mexico but was actually secretly pardoned by the Republican government of Mexico and managed to escape to El Salvador. One version says that Maximilian was replaced by someone else at the last moment, or that he was shot with salvo bullets and the emperor only pretended to be dead before he was later dispatched to Central America. A photograph of Justo Armas, who died in 1936 after his 100th birthday, does indeed show a likeness to the ill-fated emperor, although the comparison is difficult because Armas was at a very advanced age in the only available picture.

Did Maximilian escape his execution? Viennese historian and expert on the Second Mexican Empire, Konrad Ratz, firmly believes that this is a legend. Ratz has been able to demonstrate that Maximilian was inside his cell up to the last minute before his execution. He wrote several letters with his last dispositions from his prison cell. Though there are no photographs of the shooting, Ratz published a drawing of the execution as described by François Albert, an eyewitness, and the illustration is at the Royal Army Museum of Brussels. In Ratz´s opinion, Justo Armas was certainly an Austrian, and probably an officer of Maximilian's volunteer army. "Of the six thousand members of that troop, only 3,600 returned with the French and another 800 did so after the fall of the Empire. The rest…stayed in Mexico or went to other countries," Ratz writes. The objects in Armas´s possession must have sadly come from the looting carried out both by Mexicans and the men loyal to Maximilian when the empire fell.

The Treasure of the "Vita"

The Nevado de Toluca (The Snowed Peak of Toluca) is the fourth highest in Mexico and one of the country's many active volcanoes. Its summit is formed by several crests that rise about 15,000 feet above sea level. They are covered with snow almost all year round, but they harbor several lakes of ice water. It´s no wonder that someone thought of the bottom of one of those lakes as the place where no one would ever search for a treasure, given that they were practically inaccessible until the 1940s. But in the words of Sherlock Holmes, "What one man can hide, another can discover."

A picture of Nevado de Toluca

One of Nevado de Toluca's lakes

In this case, it was Dr. Miguel Guzman, a mountaineer and deep-sea diver, who got lucky. In 1963, he started to climb the heights of the Nevado de Toluca, and on his journey he found several tin boxes similar to coffins, antique clocks, and religious objects, much to his surprise. When Dr. Guzman commented on his finds at a lecture entitled *Diving on the Roof of the World*, one of the attendees stood up and confided to him that when he was a child, his father had taken him to the heights of the Nevado de Toluca. There, he asked the peasants to go into the lake, from which they removed jewels, rubies, and emeralds, which they gave to his father in exchange for a few pesos.

The stories of Spanish ships filled with gold that lay at the bottom of the Caribbean are well-known, but how could a treasure end up inside an icy lake at one of the highest summits of Mexico? As it turned out, back in 1939, the Spanish Republic, in exile, sent its treasure of jewels, archaeological treasures, gold, and religious objects to Mexico from the cathedrals of Toledo and Tortosa. Among the artifacts was one of the Christ nails. The treasure was valued at $7 million at the time. [viii] Several pieces came from the National Archaeological Museum of Spain, and divers brought up more than 30 cases of tin with an inscription that read "Pawnshop of Madrid." Republicans had filled about 150 sacks of valuable items and sent them to Mexico on a ship called *Vita*. The precious objects arrived at a secret home in Mexico City, were stocked in the basement, and melted or sold to collectors to raise money for the Republican cause. Apparently, someone stole them and hid them in the most inaccessible place he could think of: the bottom of a lake atop a volcano. Just how he took them up there remains a question.

Today, Spain regrets the loss and destruction of this important part of its artistic heritage. Recently, the University of Barcelona published *The Treasure of the Vita*, which issued a harsh judgment on the Spanish republicans: "To begin with, never a legitimate government had appropriated the possibility of confiscating a part of the treasure of the state they represented to turn them into assets, nor a group of politicians who proclaimed themselves as representatives of the popular will," writes author Fernando Gracia. The treasure of the Vita was "a true fortune at the time," but according to Gracia, the people who bought the diamonds or coins will remain silent because they would have to give explanations.

The Valley of the Seven Luminaries

The town of Santiago, in the state of Guanajuato, is located in the central part of Mexico, nearly 200 miles north of the capital. It was founded by the Spaniards at the beginning of the 17th century, but the area had been inhabited many years before. The town doesn't look very different from the others sprinkled in that region of Mexico, except when one glimpses the landscape from above on an airplane, or with Google Maps. From the air, it almost looks like a photograph of the Moon, as the area appears to have been bombarded by asteroids. These craters, likely the remains of seven to nine volcanoes that have been extinct for centuries, are known to locals as "sockets" or "jewels." The almost circular shape of the craters, with their abrupt edges and flat centers of up to almost a mile long, make this corner an ideal place to imagine what it would be like to walk on a lunar landscape, especially inside its craters. Diving and other aquatic sports are practiced in the larger ones. Others can be accessed only through a 1,500 foot tunnel, built to take advantage of the once fresh but now salted water in the craters. In the crater called "De las Flores," water springs from the cliffs. Others have lakes that change color according to the season of the year. Most of them contain prehistoric paintings, and one of them contains vestiges of a pre-Hispanic ceremonial center. Many are connected by underground tunnels.

This would be enough to make the Valley of the Seven Luminaries, declared a protected natural area since 1997, an interesting corner of Mexico, but there are also many legends about the place. In particular, one legend has it that the Yuriria lake has its own sea monster, a cousin of sorts of the famous Nessie of Scotland, which the locals call Water Chupacabras. The inhabitants of the lake began to suspect the Water Chupacabras' presence when they found a multitude of dead birds, each of them with a single bite in their necks. In 2010, it was reported that a man named Pedro Hernandez de la Copalera had seen the animal stuck to a dead heron and he killed it with a slingshot. "The animal had slimy skin and looked like a rodent called tuza, but without the skin, and it smelled badly." He picked it up with a branch and took it to the town of La Angostura, where a friend took a couple of pictures. Later, they threw it back to the lake.

A picture with the lake in the background

The other peculiarity in the Valley of the Seven Luminaries, and a much more conspicuous one, is its production of giant vegetables. There have been photographs of people carrying 33 pound onions, celery bushes measuring 3 feet long, and leaves of chard double the size. In the 1970s, the first lady of Mexico took Uri Geller - the famous Israeli magician – to the site to get his opinion. What the illusionist and self-styled psychic told her about giant vegetables remains unknown, but perhaps his spoon bent when he tried to eat them.

The Silent Zone

Durango is located in northwestern Mexico and is a well-known film location, with Raoul Walsh filming *Pancho Villa* there, followed by several Western movies shot in its fantastic landscapes in the 1960s. But among the locals, the state is known for a desert area called the Silent Zone, the closest thing Mexico has to a Roswell. Road signs announce when one is entering this extensive, arid zone, located in a part of the Mapimí Biosphere Reserve that was under the sea in prehistoric times. Many archaeological remains of marine animals have been found.

The Silent Zone has birthed several legends, but one thing is certain: on July 11, 1970, the United States Army was testing a rocket named Athena V-123-D in the state of Utah as a part of the Advanced Ballistic Reentry System (ABRES) program, when the men in charge suddenly realized – no doubt much to their chagrin - that the device had gone off-course and was heading towards Mexico. Exacerbating the situation, the Athena was carrying a significant charge of radioactive cobalt in its nose, a material used to enhance radioactive fallout with the intention of contaminating large areas of land. Fortunately for everyone, the device fell over one of the most desolate of Mexico's deserts, and the Mexican government, which may well have considered it a military aggression, was very understanding, even allowing a team of American experts to go to the Durango Desert to recover the remains of the missile after the Mexican Army quickly cordoned off the site. After apologizing, the United States took its rocket pieces away, as well as the radioactive material and several tons of soil that were supposedly contaminated. The U.S. even built a special highway from Durango to Utah.

The matter could have ended there, but people started reporting strange incidents in the area afterwards. First, an inhabitant of the village of Ceballos said he´d found a spot in which a radio could not be heard. Others said they´d found sites near the impact where it was impossible to hear another person talking, even if the person was directly in front of them. They also said that compasses went crazy in the Silent Zone. A short time later, UFO sightings began, followed by the abnormal growth of plants and animals, as well as luminous phenomena. The most popular explanation is that the magnetic waves of the Earth had been inverted there, and that "a kind of magnetic cone was created in the region which causes ionizations in the atmosphere that block the transmission of radio waves." [ix] Curiously, hardly anyone mentions or remembers the missile and its radioactive load, which seems seem to have fallen into its own silent zone.

Is this the stuff of truth or fiction? It´s certainly possible the locals invented the phenomena, in a way similar to Roswell, to attract tourists - hippies, witch-doctors, peyoteros, and other tribes and groups - to a place that otherwise would be a forgotten wilderness on the map. Some of the most serious teams that have searched the area haven't been able to find the supposed spot where radios go silent, compasses go crazy, and the voices of people become inaudible. The locals´ explanation is that the area is actually a spot that constantly changes places, and that it is a matter of luck to find it. What is not easy to find is a neighbor as sympathetic as Mexico, which seemingly figured out how to turn a profit out of being attacked with a radioactive missile.

Paricutin

One Saturday afternoon, a humble peasant named Dionisio Pulido was preparing his cornfield when suddenly, at 5:30 p.m., he heard a noise below the earth and saw smoke emerging from his furrows. Curiosity flaring in his eyes, he approached and saw a crack open in the ground from which a column of smoke came out. His wife went to see, too, but both covered their noses in disgust because the smell was unbearable. Not knowing what to do with the six-foot crack in the middle of their field, they went home and turned in time to see the most incredible spectacle a human being could ever see: the field began to rise and form a cone that reached three meters high. "I saw how the earth swelled and rose two or three meters high," recalls the farmer, "and a kind of smoke or fine dust, gray as ashes, began to rise in a portion of the crevice that I had not seen previously. More smoke began to rise with a whiff and there was a smell of sulfur. Then I became very frightened and tried to help the yoke of the ox. I was so stunned I didn´t know just what to do or what to think, and I could not find my wife, my son or my animals. At last I came to my senses and I remembered the Sacred Lord of Miracles. I shouted, 'Blessed Lord of Miracles, you brought me into this world."

Dionisio fled in terror to Paricutin, the nearest town, in the state of Michoacan. Unbeknownst to him, he had just seen the birth of a volcano. It was February 20, 1943.

For days, the villagers had noticed strange things. For example, they had heard thunder but saw no clouds, and they had heard hissing sounds and perceived strange smells. That night in February, unsure of what was happening, they kept hearing noises "like the surge of the sea" and saw "flames in the sky…that burst like golden marigolds, and a rain like artificial fire fell to the ground." Early in the morning, as soon as there was light, the men went to Dionisio´s field and gaped at what they saw: the cone of a volcano grew before their very eyes and was throwing rocks and smoke. By the end of that Sunday, it was already over 150 feet high, and in the following week, it reached double the size before it began to expel lava. In March, the eruption grew furious and continued to do so over the next nine years.

Pictures of the volcano erupting in 1943

In 1952, after the volcano finally stopped growing and the eruption ended, the town of Paricutin was completely buried under the lava. A year later, only the towers of the church of the neighboring village, Parangaricutiro, emerged from the hardened rock, a silent witness to the first time scientists were able to observe the birth of a volcano and document all its stages from birth to extinction.

A modern picture of the Paricutin volcano today

San Juan Parangaricutiro Church

Paricutin attracted millions of scientists from all over the world and produced thousands of photographs. The Smithsonian National Museum of Natural History later noted in a publication, "The birth of a volcano was exciting not only to scientists. It generated tremendous interest among the populace at large. An image of Foshag was featured in *Life* magazine with the smoking volcano in the background. Pan American planes between Los Angeles and Mexico City reportedly diverted from their regular route in order to be able to show passengers the new volcano."

As the world's youngest volcano, CNN named it one of the seven natural wonders of the world, and it was a natural laboratory for geologists from around the world. Not surprisingly, it also sparked a new interest in volcanology, art, and photography.

Dionisio died in 1949, seven years after the volcano´s birth. "He was the only human being who owned a volcano and who owned nothing," wrote the great Mexican writer, Jose Revueltas, for posterity.

A Town of Werewolves

Stories of humans that turn into wolves go all the way back to Ancient Greece, but it was during the Middle Ages when they became a firmly embedded element in European folklore. The story of *Little Red Riding Hood* may contain traces of mankind's fear of werewolves.

How did this myth originate? There is an unusual disease in humans called hypertrichosis, which consists of excessive growth and the intense presence of hair on the face and body, though it´s a very rare condition. In fact, one might say it is as rare as the werewolf itself; only 50 cases of congenital *Hypertrichosis lanuginosa* have been recorded over the last 500 years, with those unlucky people having their body completely covered with hair. The other variety, called *Generalized hypertrichosis*, causes a "werewolf-like face" in the males of a family.

Of the 50 cases reported, more than half have occurred in Central Mexico around a town called Loreto (about 400 miles north of Mexico City), which folklore has baptized as the Town of the Werewolf. In the past, scientists have documented cases of hypertrichosis, but the disease has always been accompanied by serious physical disorders, such as mental handicaps and skeletal abnormalities. Conversely, the Mexican "werewolves" are completely normal and nice people, except for their wooly appearance.

For years, the male members of the families of Loreto have found jobs in Mexico's circuses and have been invited to participate in European circuses as well. Mexican werewolves–who became universally known in the 1970s, thanks to television–show an abnormal growth of hair all over the face, neck, and upper body, covering their cheeks, nose, and even their eyelids. People suffering from the disease even have more hair than chimpanzees or gorillas on those parts of the body.

Dr. José Cantú, head of Genetics at the Mexican Institute for Social Security in Guadalajara, thinks that in that family - and in other well-documented cases of hypertrichosis throughout history - a gene dormant for millions of years may have been awakened. "The researchers do not yet have the precise gene isolated, but merely know its approximate location, on the bottom half of the X chromosome. They found the location by examining the genetic material of a large Mexican family, whose members may be the only humans known to have this particular mutation."

No one knows why this occurrence exists in Mexico, but it's well-known that ancient Mexicans invented the myth of the *nagual*, a man who can turn into a dog or a coyote. The best known case of the disease is that of Julia Pastrana, an indigenous woman born in Sinaloa at the beginning of the 19th century. Mrs. Pastrana was completely covered with long, thick, shiny, black hair, and had a prominent lower jaw. Pastrana, whose appearance had the characteristics of a prehistoric woman, was even commented upon by Charles Darwin himself. Unfortunately, she was mercilessly exploited by her own unscrupulous husband, Theodore Lent, even after her death, when he had her and her baby mummified and displayed in a glass cabinet; Julia Pastrana died in Moscow in 1860, four days after giving birth to a child with the same disease.

A picture of Pastrana's embalmed body

The Weeping Woman

When the great Tenochtitlan fell in 1521, it ushered in the Colonial Era in Mexico. The commencement was not easy. When Cortés and his allies arrived in the capital of the Aztec empire, there were about 25 million inhabitants in what is now Mexico, but 100 years later, only 1-1.5 million natives remained, most of them having perished in the war or killed by diseases brought by the Europeans. Some also died due to the forced labor to which they were subjected.

During the years following the Conquest, wrote the great connoisseur of the Colonial Period, Artemio del Valle Arizpe, the inhabitants of Mexico City began to hear a disturbing presence that roamed the streets at night. It was a woman who cried with a prolonged and pitiful lament that ran through the city. "Mexico was terrified by those anguished groans. When they heard, many went out to ascertain who the being who cried in such a mournful and painful way was. Several people affirmed that it was an otherworldly being, because a human howl was no longer heard at a distance of two or three blocks away, but with its strength this one crossed a great distance and came clear, distinctive, to all ears with her bitter lament. Many went out to investigate, some died of fright, others went bersek," writes Del Valle. As soon as dusk approached, people locked themselves in their houses, and if they heard the cries, they said: "Here comes the Weeping Woman, la Llorona."

According to tradition, in the middle of the 16th century, the woman walked through the downtown streets of present-day Mexico City, went around the squares and plazas, and stopped at the *Zocalo* or main square, where the Metropolitan Cathedral stands. There she let out her most aggrieved cry and immediately knelt and turned to the east, kissing the ground. When she was done, she left, vanishing at the outskirts of town. This happened every night until, according to Del Valle Arizpe, the apparition stopped appearing in the first years of the 17th century. The writer also related that several hypotheses were advanced about the woman's identity, with people speculating that she was the ghost of an unfaithful wife who couldn't bear her guilt, that the woman had been murdered by her husband, or that she was a woman who had drowned her own children in the river and then committed suicide after being rejected by her lover. The *Llorona* always repeated the same lamentation: "Oh, my children, your destruction has already come...Oh, my children, where will I take you so that you don't lose yourselves?"

Legends of weeping women can also be found in different cultures, but only in Mexico is it said to represent a historical fact: the destruction of the ancient pre-Hispanic civilization at the hands of the Spanish conquistadors. For this same reason, the most popular explanation of the Llorona's identity, whether it is a real ghost, a figment of the imagination, or a projection of the anguish of Mexicans, is that she is Malintzin, Cortés' native interpreter. As a result of her position, she is viewed as the female traitor who, in helping the conquistador, caused the misery of all of her race and the children in her land. [x] Curiously, in those years, another narrative of a mythical woman appeared, a celestial being announcing the end of one civilization and the beginning of another: the Virgin of Guadalupe.

Tlatelolco´s Ghosts

Most of those interested in the history of ancient Mexico have heard of Tenochtitlan, built in the middle of the Lake of Texcoco, but the Aztec capital had a sister city, on the same lake, called Tlatelolco, an important market upon which the great Tenochititlan depended. Today a borough of Mexico City, the site could well be remembered for its terrible luck, as two of the most remembered and lamented massacres in Mexico´s history happened there.

It was in Tletelolco where the Aztecs fought the last battle against the Spaniards in 1521. That August, Cortés undertook a final offensive with his army of more than 150,000 men, and the siege lasted 76 days. After a historic resistance, Tlatelolco fell and Cortés set fire to the city, killing its 40,000 defenders. A poem written by a survivor expresses the pain and disappointment of its inhabitants:

"Giver of Life, indeed, we your people will perish.

You have raged and indeed we went in misery, we people.

We saw the affliction in the Place of Knowledge.

You dispersed and destroyed your people in Tlatelolco.

Affliction upon affliction come fall down in the Place of Revelation.

Teardrops fall, crying protection in Tlatelolco.

Smoke rises, fog spreads there. You caused it, oh Giver of Life.

Weep and realize this, oh friends:

you have abandoned the Mexican people.

The water is bitter and the food is bitter."

The Spaniards eventually built another city on top of Tlatelolco´s ruins, a city with European styles, but more than four centuries later, Tlatelolco was the scene of another massacre. In the Square of the Three Cultures, in the midst of student protests following the Paris Spring of 1968, a crowd of students gathered in a peaceful demonstration. At a signal, the army surrounded the crowd, entering from several sides to the square, and shot them. The death toll is still a secret, and nearly 50 years later there are still people demanding justice.

The suffering of people Tlatelolco does not end there either. In 1985, several departmental buildings collapsed after an earthquake registering 8.1 on the Richter Scale, leaving hundreds of families under the rubble. Is it a coincidence that, among so much death and desolation, the inhabitants of the buildings in Tlatelolco constantly report that they hear sobs, calls for help, sounds of children playing, and in particular, shots of high caliber weapons?

One of the most recurrent stories is about a girl who died in the earthquake and appeared in the corridors of buildings to leave a message to her parents. The most notorious case with funny undertones is the ghost of a young dancer who was seen for several days by dozens of people at 2:00 in the morning. The chronicler of that borough of Mexico, Cuauhtémoc Abarca, reported that the ghost was "a young man dressed in white sports shirt and pants. He ran through the archaeological zone and returned to (the walls of) the church, began a modern dance in the atrium, then went back to church. He ran so fast that he seemed to float. After twenty minutes, he disappeared." The chronicler admitted how implausible his story sounded, but he said many people saw the boy, and that once the neighbors came to wake him up so he could see him with his own eyes. When a woman finally approached the young boy to tell him he no longer belonged to this world, the apparitions stopped.

In 2009, a team of archaeologists, led by Salvador Guilliem, found 49 human skeletons ritually buried in the area, each one wrapped in large maguey cactus leaves. All of them were warriors, but among the remains was the skeleton of a young man with a ring on his finger, possibly a symbol of status. Could he have been the phantom dancer?

The Planchada

Possibly the most famous ghost of Mexico City is the Planchada (the Neat Nurse), a nurse that appears in the old Juarez Hospital, located at the historical center of the city. Those who have seen her agree that, unlike other ghosts, she stands out for her beauty, serenity, and above all else, the pureness of her uniform, which is impeccably ironed, without a single stain to break its whiteness. Both patients and medical personnel describe her as a young, tall, blonde woman (an unusual feature among Mexican women) who steps into the rooms during the night shift to give medication to the sick, specifically when the shift nurse has fallen asleep. In some cases, the Planchada awakens nurses who have nodded off. After the 1985 earthquake, which destroyed much of downtown Mexico City, including a part of the Juarez Hospital, the young lady was seen by many injured as she wandered the medical center's corridors.

Older nurses declare that the Neat Nurse really existed. Her real name was Eulalia, and she was a young, pretty assistant who fell in love with a doctor working at the Juarez Hospital. The romance flourished, but one day the boyfriend had to move to the city of Guadalajara, promising Eulalia he'd eventually come back for her. However, she got news that the man had married another woman in Western Mexico. Shattered and broken-hearted, Eulalia became rude and careless to the point that one of her patients died due to her lack of care. Eulalia grew old and died waiting for the boyfriend that never came back. It is for this reason she is condemned to roam the Juarez Hospital and properly fulfill the duties she neglected whilst alive.

The Juarez Hospital began as a church, but it was adapted as a hospital in 1847, when the United States Army occupied Mexico's capital. In view of the urgency of treating thousands of wounded, the church was transformed into a medical facility. The soldiers of the Battle of Churubusco were the first to be attended to there, three days after the conflagration, on August 23, 1847. The hospital continues to operate to this day and has been celebrated for many medical achievements in the country's history. It was there where the first radiograph was taken, the second blood transfusion center in the Americas was installed, and the country's first blood bank was established in 1942.

It's possible that the legend of the ghost has a historical kernel. Apparently, the real Planchada, blonde and slim, was an American nurse who came with the U.S. Army, and at night, she moved secretly to impoverished Mexican hospitals to help her fellow nurses take care of the dying. According to various testimonies, it was around this time the legend of the blonde nurse began to take shape. "In the main office of this hospital, where strangely entering is very restricted, even for those who work there, there's a painting in one of the walls; that picture, according to the inmates of the hospital, depicts this nurse about whom almost nothing is known, where she came from, when she entered the hospital or how she died; it's only known that she was a beautiful woman, with short blond hair, quiet, but above all strict, always in starched white uniform, walking up the aisles" (Gaxiola, 2015).

The Witches of Tlaxcala

In the middle of 20th century, a strange phenomenon turned up in the Mexican state of Tlaxcala when several infant death certificates cited "sucked by the witch" as the cause of death. The belief in the *tlahuelpuchi*, a kind of witch who sucks the blood of babies, is widespread in that part of Mexico. According to their inhabitants, especially in rural areas, thalhuelpuchi women are normal-looking people who were born cursed. They live incognito with their human families, who prefer not to disclose their identity, not only to protect them but because the one who causes a witch's death will perish in the same way. These women change shape at night, leaving their legs in the kitchen in the form of a cross, enter other homes appearing as either a vulture or a turkey, and feed on the blood of babies. Women born with the curse only realize their situation when they reach puberty, a time when the adolescent develops an insatiable appetite for human blood, which comes as a shock to the whole family. Their condition stays with the woman for life, but it's difficult to for someone who does not live with her to detect it.

Intrigued by the hundreds of reports of babies "sucked by the witch," between 1959 and 1966, anthropologist Hugo G. Nutini investigated about 300 cases of infant deaths in Tlaxcala, examining about 50 corpses of children. Just a few years earlier, in 1954, Tlaxcala State had issued a provision requiring families to inform the medical authorities of such cases. Nutini was able to verify the belief went back several generations. The families, Nutini learned, never denounced their daughters, but in some cases, their witch condition "was so unmistakable" that they were lynched. When this happened, the townspeople amputated her fingers and other sensory organs and disposed of the body far from the village, without ceremony.

During his investigation, Nutini was able to confirm the lynching of at least one tlahuelpuchi. In August 1961, while working in the village of San Diego, Tlaxcala, one of her most reliable sources came running to inform him that a woman had just been accused of being tlahuelpuchi in a nearby community, that she'd been killed the night before, and her corpse was in a ravine. The researcher persuaded one of the inhabitants to take him to see the body. He wanted to confirm that people could actually kill an alleged witch in her human form and not, as he supposed, as an animal. Nutini indeed found a human body, totally naked, "most of her bones broken, and her body a formless mass of bruises and wounds. Her eyes had been plucked from the sockets, her ears, nose, tongue and lips had been totally severed, and her ten fingers had been cut clean." (Nutini, 1993). Some informants told him that these executions were more common than anyone thought, but that they were not reported because in Tlaxcala, as in any part of the world, killing a human being is a very serious crime. The investigator found that these homicides had occurred during periods of crisis, such as when more than three infants in a village appeared dead in their cribs. In a study published with Horacio Fábrega in 1994 in *Culture, Medicine and Psychiatry*, a peer reviewed journal, the scholars explained that the belief in blood-sucking witches was a way for parents to assimilate the immense pain caused by sudden infant death, an obvious cultural stressor.

Haunted Houses in Mexico City

Is there another part of the world with more "haunted houses" than Mexico City? For some reason, the so-called City of Palaces is also known as the City of Ghosts, where they are especially abundant in the historic center. Two important facts have contributed to this infamous label: human sacrifices performed by the Aztecs—archaeological sites with up to 60,000 human skulls have been found—and immolations at the Alameda Central (a kind of Central Park in Mexico City) during the Spanish Inquisition.

Thus, it would not be unusual to find reported sightings of ghosts in Mexico City if, as Algernon Blackwood wrote, ghosts are the result of misfortunes, "chiefly the evil emotions that are able to leave their photographs on surrounding scenes and objects; and whoever heard of a place haunted by a noble deed, or of beautiful and lovely ghosts revisiting the glimpses of the moon?" Whether truth or fiction in nature, many people have reported apparitions, especially in the Palace of Lecumberri (now the General Archive of the Nation), once a dreaded prison where well-known and unknown people were tortured and killed, many of them during the dirty war against students in the 1960s.

The old Palace of the Inquisition (now the Medical Museum of Mexico) has an even worse reputation—and more ghosts. Built in 1732, the dreaded Spanish institution operated until 1821. The Majestic Hotel—right in Mexico City's main square—is famous because many guests and countless employees have seen an elegantly dressed man wearing a top hat in the hotel's mirrors, and a child known as Pablito appears in Restaurant Ixchel. The child is supposedly the ghost of a minor who died years ago when he fell down the patio stairs.

Another report worthy of consideration is the ghost girl who appears at the Mexico City airport, which seems at first blush to be an unlikely place. The girl is about seven years old, holds a ball, and asks people to tie the ribbons of her shoes before disappearing. She's so popular that there are several videos on YouTube, posted by people who have supposedly managed to capture the ghost on video. A photograph of the girl peering out the window of an abandoned plane went viral and reached the news websites of several Latin American countries.

The most infamous—and lucrative—ghost story of the capital is possibly the so-called "Cañitas House," a normal-looking house located northeast of the city. The case spawned a book in 1995, many lectures, and a horrendous motion picture in 2007 (with a Rotten Tomatoes rating of 17%). The story began in 1982, when a girl named Norma, desperate to communicate with her dead boyfriend, started playing with a Ouija board with his brothers. During the session, one of the kids begins to convulse and say in a voice that was not his own that they had unleashed something uncontrollable, and after a few years, almost all of the participants of that session were dead due to strange circumstances.

Carlos Trejo, the house's owner, published a book about his experience living there, and he revealed that there was a cemetery of monks of Tacubaya under the place. However, no historian or archaeologist has given credit to his claims. Moreover, the alleged victims showed up later, in perfect health, to claim part of the book's royalties. The book is full of contradictions and the film was lampooned by the critics. One investigator who agreed to look into the case concluded that the only thing he had found was "a broken, stricken family… and the claim that the house was haunted functioned as an emotional lifeguard, where they found a justification for their existence and the unfortunate events they had suffered."

The Soccer Wars

Soccer devotees can attest that Mexican and Latin American fans are some of the most picturesque crowds; not only do they shout and curse while dressed in extravagant costumes, they also aggressively celebrate their victories and cry when their team loses. On one occasion, a war between Honduras and El Salvador nearly broke out due to a soccer game, in an embarrassing incident known as The Football War. [xi]

In fact, the habit of mixing football and death is not new in the region. The Mayans invented a variety of soccer played by striking the ball, not with the feet but with the right hip, right elbow, and/or right knee. The goalposts were impossibly small, in the form of two stone rings protruding from the side walls of the court. In the Mayan language, the sport was known as *pok a pok*, "due to the funny sound that the ball made on the floors and walls of the courts, or when players hit it with their forearms or hips." [xii] Some assume the game was a form of "playing war," or that it represented the conflict between life and the underworld. The game ended as soon as the first goal was scored, an indication that it must have been extraordinarily hard to score. When the game was over, all the players on one team were sacrificed, and it's still not clear whether the sacrificial victims were the winners or the losers of the game. "The heavy, often soccer-sized ball was made from hard rubber; some scholars think that human skulls were placed inside the balls. The games were cultural spectacles followed by human sacrifices. Not everyone thinks it was the losers who were offered to the gods," wrote Michael Shapiro for the *National Geographic* in 2012. "A guide in Tikal firmly believes it was the winners."

There are several accounts of this game in stone, as well as in the *Popol Vuh*, the sacred book of the Maya, which describes the immolation of the players. Most scholars believe that the way to kill the competitors was by decapitation—beginning with the winning captain—and that his skull was used, after proper preparation, as the ball for the next game.

Whatever the case, *pok a pok* courts have been found all over Southern Mexico, which is why many Mexicans mistakenly consider themselves to be the inventors of football. Historian Fray Bernardino de Sahagun wrote in the 16th century, "They didn't play with their hands but with the buttocks. In Tenochtitlan there were four deaths at the end of each game, and after they were killed, the people dragged their bodies all over the land, and it was as if they painted the ground with their blood." Unfortunately, in Mexico, death and football are still joined in a deadly and stupid embrace. In 2016, a soccer player named Ruben Rivera Vazquez killed the referee with a blow to the head after the official gave Rivera a red card.

Brian Snelson's picture of the Great Ballcourt at Chichen Itza

The Presidents Who Spoke to Spirits

The Mexican Revolution, the wind that swept Mexico and left more than one million dead, is better known through the iconic figures of Pancho Villa and Emiliano Zapata, peasant heroes who fought for land and freedom as the heads of their arrmies. But it was Francisco Madero and Plutarco Elias Calles, Mexico's presidents in 1911 and 1924, who started it and drew the curtain, respectively. Madero was a Catholic and a conservative, while Calles was a fervent communist and atheist, but both believed in spirits, and at different stages of their lives, they tried to communicate with the dead.

Francisco I. Madero, a decent, well-educated man and student at the University of Berkeley, became interested in Spiritism during a trip to Paris when he visited the tomb of Allan Kardec, the founder of Spiritism. After that, he came to the conclusion that he himself was a medium. Nine years before the beginning of the Revolution, he became convinced that his brother Raul, who had died at the age of four, was communicating with him. He published several books on Spiritism under a pseudonym. The soon-to-be president held several spiritualist sessions at his Society of Psychic Studies of San Pedro, where he wrote several documents in trance. The spirits who spoke through Madero´s pen urged the members to "avoid playing pool and take advantage of that time to practice charity; to use the material riches bestowed by God to do good among the poor; to dominate their fleshly passions and reject vices". According to historian Anita Brenner, on one occasion the Ouija said to him, "Panchito, one day you will be the president of Mexico," which indeed happened in 1911. Unfortunately, Madero was such a weak president that even the newspapers called him a "madman who communicates with the dead." Madero was assassinated in a *coup d'etat* in 1913, at the age of 39.

Madero

At the other end of the Mexican Revolution was Plutarco Elias Calles, an angry atheist who liked to boast that "as a kid, when I was an altar boy, I stole alms to buy candy." Calles, the most anti-clerical president in Mexico's history, unleashed a religious persecution, seized church property, expelled most of the clergy from the country, and even had some of them executed. However, at the end of his life, when the country was pacified and he led a quiet life in Cuernavaca, he became interested in spirits and life after death. On one occasion, he wrote that he'd seen several ghosts in his house during the night. The proceedings of the Metapsychic Research Circle of Mexico describe that during a session, Calles saw a small child of delicate features, whom he recognized as a son of his who had died at the age of five.

Calles passed away four years after his initiation into spiritualism, but he returned—again, according to the acts of the Circle, published in 1960—to deliver several messages from the afterlife. According to the Acts, two years after his death, the most anti-religious president of Mexico appeared to members on May 20, 1947: "He greeted us with energetic hugs and coughed slightly before speaking, as he used to do in life." His last message was: "I love you with all my heart, but not with the heart that was buried in a pit on the ground, but with the heart of the spirit that will never die."

Calles

The Mummies of Guanajuato

Museums around the world are increasingly cautious with exhibits that include mummies or human body parts recovered from archaeological digs. Many advocacy groups are pushing to prohibit them out of respect for the dead, even though curators are meticulous and try to comply with good taste. But this is not so in the state of Guanajuato, Mexico, a mining town with a medieval flavor that hosts what is possibly the most frightening exhibit in the world. Known as the "Museum of the Mummies of Guanajuato," the site has been rated in several travel guides as the world's most shocking museum. Not all visitors have the stomach to finish the tour.

At the end of the 19th century, the graveyard of Santa Paola, which is next to the museum, began to require payment for the use of its above-ground crypts. The families who couldn't pay the rent had to see their dead relatives removed and thrown into a common grave. By a unique combination of factors in Guanajuato, the cemetery administrators were surprised to discover that most of the corpses had been mummified. The first mummy to be extracted almost perfectly preserved came in 1865: the corpse of a French doctor named Remigio Leroy.

For decades, the cemetery stored the mummies and allowed the curious to get an eyeful, in exchange for a small bribe. Finally, in 1958, the government of Guanajuato opened the Museum, which receives half a million visitors per year, to the public.

The museum has over 100 mummies on display. The bodies, naked and not exactly displayed with artistic sensibility, show the terrifying side of humanity´s final act. Some include victims of the Inquisition, still pierced in their bed of spears, murdered villagers, men buried alive (one can tell by the way their hands are raised that they were trying to push the cover off the coffin), and women twisted in gestures of agony, with expressions that can cause nightmares for newcomers. The museum has a special hall with mummies of newborn babies, most of them dressed as saints—Saint Martin de Porres being one of the favorites—since people believed it would facilitate their entry to heaven, especially if, as surely was the case, they died before being baptized. The site prides itself on having the world's smallest mummy, a fetus the size of a coin, found inside a woman who had been removed from her grave. The visitors can examine the unborn child with the assistance of a magnifying glass.

Several of the mummies on display have their own story, but the sources are uncertain. One of them is said to have been hanged by her husband, while another was clearly stabbed to death. There is even a severed finger that supposedly emerged from its grave to point out his murderer.

Regardless, the experience may be excessive for some. Ray Bradbury, who visited the cemetery´s catacombs in 1945, wrote, "The experience so wounded and terrified me, I could hardly wait to flee Mexico. I had nightmares about dying and having to remain in the halls of the dead with those propped and wired bodies."

The Santa Muerte

Santa Muerte Bianca

Possibly one of the strangest spectacles that can be seen in some parts of Mexico, especially in the capital´s slums, are the temples and masses celebrated in honor of the Santa Muerte (the Holy Death), the cadaveric saint, a kind of negative image of the Virgin of Guadalupe. In the north of the country, truck drivers find altars dedicated to Santa Muerte by the side of the roads, especially in regions scourged by violence and drug trafficking. But it´s especially in the Tepito neighborhood, one of the poorest and most dangerous, where foreign anthropologists are racking their brains in an effort to explain the flood of people who come to prostrate themselves before a skeleton dressed as a saint. They touch her clothes, leave her offerings, and above all else, ask her for favors, usually dark ones, such as protection during a robbery, to be able to cross the U.S. border successfully, or even to help kill an enemy without being caught by the police.

Erroneously, many observers link this cult to the traditional festivities of the Day of the Dead in Mexico, but while they look alike, they are completely different things. The cult of Santa Muerte is rather recent, while the Day of the Dead festivities are more family entertainment, the

Mexican version of Halloween. The cult of the Santa Muerte arose in the Tepito neighborhood and prisons of the capital during the mid-20th century. American anthropologist Oscar Lewis, who lived in Tepito in order to develop his concept of "culture of poverty," mentions it in his classic novel *Los hijos de Sánchez*. In the book, Martha, one of the characters, says, "My sister Antonia…told me that when husbands are straying, you can pray to Santa Muerte. It is a novena that should be prayed at twelve o'clock." The people who practiced this strange ritual did it privately in a room of their house, where they had an effigy of this skeletal saint, sometimes the size of a real person.

In the middle of the 1990s, the Holy Death made her transition to the public sphere. The rumor spread that the Santa Muerte granted many miracles, that belief in her protected from danger, or at least that when the time came, the follower would experience a good death (without pain). In 2001, a woman named Enriqueta Romero, who until then had made her income selling *quesadillas* (tacos with cheese), put an altar to the Santa Muerte outside her house, in Tepito. The "skinny´s" popularity took everyone by surprise. In the beginning, passers-by stopped to leave flowers and candles. Then the faithful—who happened to be legion—started coming from other neighborhoods until the woman decided to organize a Catholic-styled ritual in the street. Now, even the priests of the "Church of the Holy Death" (not recognized by the State) celebrate weddings.

The scholars have attributed the emergence and rapid expansion of the cult of the Santa Muerte to Mexico´s growing violence, to people´s fear of suffering a violent death, and the influence of criminal groups that have adopted her not only as their trademark but as a way to intimidate. Meanwhile, big corporations that go wherever profit is present are rubbing their hands. In most popular markets, and even in big outlets like Wal-Mart and online stores like Amazon, it´s possible to buy effigies and candles of all colors to be used in the rituals of the Santa Muerte. People can even get black candles, the ones used when asking for an enemy´s death.

The Black Mass of Catemaco

Mexico may be one of the most Catholic countries in the world; after all, it houses the second most visited Catholic shrine on the planet after the Vatican. Even politicians and first ladies have turned there for the help of sorcerers and mediums. Mexican *popular* Catholicism is one of the most flexible, to the point of combining orthodox beliefs with celebrations for the dead, veneration to a skeleton called "La Santa Muerte," and visits to a town of sorcerers who celebrate a black mass, not in secret but as one of the main tourist attractions in Catemaco, the "Town of the Witches ."

Santeria and witchcraft is so time-honored in this remote village that municipal authorities have at least 20 people to guide tourists to the houses of healers or witches, most of them male. A former governor of the state of Veracruz, where Catemaco is located, even proposed (unsuccessfully) to establish a school for sorcerers. Although there are witches - the name given to people who practice some form on non-conventional medicine - throughout Mexico, it´s commonly accepted that those in Catemaco are the most powerful.

People go to Catemaco to find a magic cure when doctors say there is no cure, to ask for success in business, or to conquer the heart of a loved one, but the place is also open to young people who wish to study Santeria and receive instructions from the oldest and wisest witches. "Catemaco is known far and wide as the city of witches, where students of white magic and the dark arts practice their trade openly and proudly, and are, in fact, in great demand by visitors from across Mexico and the world who travel there for their professional services." [xiii] The hundreds of visitors—Mexicans and foreigners alike—who go to Catemaco to take part in its famous black mass are not exactly uneducated folks either; in fact, celebrities, artists, athletes and even rising politicians have also participated in the search for amulets, whether it is to win the next World Cup or the next election.

Beside the lake of Catemaco, on the first Friday of March at midnight, the great sorcerer lights several torches and candles, marking the perimeter where the black mass will be held. A star of six peaks made of fire is lit. Then, the sorcerer sacrifices a black hen, representing evil, and he begins the rite. The attendants who have paid the entrance price go one at a time to request their remedies and cures, sit in a chair placed in the middle of a Star of David, and have the sorcerer act upon them. The people must repeat the spells the witch recites, and men must remove their shirts to be sprayed with water. Minor witches on the sides perform simpler cures with branches and leaves.

In Catemaco, a town with 8,000 homes, there are more than 230 houses of sorcerers or shamans, which undoubtedly makes it the city with more witches per capita in the world. Most of its inhabitants go to a witch before seeing a doctor.

What is the origin of this exotic practice in this corner of Mexico? The answer may come from colonial times. Catemaco remained within the lands of the Marquisate of the Valley of Oaxaca that was granted to Cortés for his services to the Spanish crown. Cortés planted tobacco, coffee, and sugar cane and imported black slaves, who brought Santeria from Africa. [xiv] Eventually, the black slaves rebelled, and, led by a chief named Yanga, they fled their masters and established villages in the interior of Veracruz. The black side of Catemaco may have nothing to do with evil forces, but rather, with memories of freedom.

Online Resources

Other mysterious titles by Charles River Editors & Sean McLachlan

Other titles about Mexico on Amazon

Bibliography

Brenner, Anita, (2010). *The Wind that Swept Mexico: The History of the Mexican Revolution of 1910-1942*. USA: University of Texas Press.

Esquinca, Bernardo, *et al.*, (2013). *Ciudad Fantasma. Relato Fantástico de la Ciudad de México*. México: Editorial Almadía.

González Gaxiola, Francisco, *et al*, (2015). *Literatura 1. Tercer Semestre*. México: Colegio de Bachilleres del Estado de Sonora.

Hatcher Childress, David, (1992). *Lost Cities of North & Central America*. USA:

Adventures Unlimited Press.

Nutini, Hugo G.; John M. Roberts, (1993). *Bloodsucking Witchcraft. An Epistemological Study of Anthropomorphic Supernaturalism in Rural Tlaxcala*. USA: University of Arizona Press

Ratz, Konrad, (2008). *Tras las huellas de un desconocido. Nuevos datos y aspectos de Maximiliano de Habsburgo*. México: CONACULTA-INAH

Saldívar Arellano, Juan Manuel, (2010). *Nuevas formas de adoración y culto: La construcción social de la Santería en Catemaco, Veracruz*. México: Visionnet Ediciones.

Vázquez-Lozano, Gustavo, (2016). *The Santa Muerte: The Origins, History, and Secrets of the Mexican Folk Saint*. USA: Charles River Editors.

Vázquez-Lozano, Gustavo, (2016). *The Virgin of Guadalupe: The History and Legacy of One of the Catholic Church's Most Venerated Images*. USA: Charles River Editors.

Free Books by Charles River Editors

We have brand new titles available for free most days of the week. To see which of our titles are currently free, click on this link.

Discounted Books by Charles River Editors

---

[i] Also called "of Tepeyac" for the place of the apparitions.

[ii] Which didn´t prevent the film, in a classic example of the contradictory nature of the Mexicans, to become a blockbuster.

[iii] In this case "ermita" denotes not a shrine but just a marker or a little altar in uninhabited areas.

[iv] As was the case in Fatima during World War I, and the Virgin of Medjugorje in the former Yugoslavia, shortly before the ethnic wars that fractured the region.

[v] The idea dates back to the middle of the seventeenth century.

[vi] The rest of Maximilian´s men had left to defend Mexico City.

[vii] At the end of his life, Lopez, who was always considered a Judas, told German writer Ernst Below that his purpose had been to facilitate the Emperor´s escape, but that Maximilian had stubbornly preferred to fall in the battlefield than running away. Lopez was not taken prisoner when Queretaro fell. He kept his freedom and allegedly received 15 thousand gold pesos.

[viii] Mexico´s president Lázaro Cárdenas actively supported the Spanish Republican cause.

[ix] *La fascinante zona del silencio (Durango)*, México Desconocido. Retrieved on November 10, 2016 from https://www.mexicodesconocido.com.mx/la-fascinante-zona-del-silencio-durango.html

[x] Malinche was one of several slave women given to Hernan Cortes by the natives of Tabasco in 1519. She played a role in the Spanish conquest of the Aztec Empire, acting as an interpreter, advisor, lover, and intermediary for Hernán Cortes. She became Cortes´ lover and gave birth to his first son.

[xi] There were actually deeper economic and agrarian reasons, but the beginning of the military hostilities between the two countries began while violence erupted in a soccer game between fans of Honduras and El Salvador.

[xii] *El juego de pelota de Chichén Itzá*, México Desconcido. Retrieved on November 10, 2016 from

https://www.mexicodesconocido.com.mx/el-juego-de-pelota-de-chichen-itza-yucatan.html

[xiii] *Catemaco, Mexico: Land of the Wizard King*, retrieved on November 10, 2016 from http://mexicolesstraveled.com/catemaco.htm

[xiv] Unlike the US, Mexico didn´t become a society based on slavery, although some black slaves entered the country, but in small numbers. Today only 1.2% of Mexico's population has significant African ancestry.

Made in the USA
Lexington, KY
23 March 2019